What Happens When We Recycle

Water?

Jillian Powell

W

FRANKLIN WATTS

LONDON · SYDNEY

This edition copyright © Franklin Watts 2014

Franklin Watts
338 Euston Rd
London NW1 3BH

Franklin Watts Australia
Level 17/207 Kent Street
Sydney NSW 2000

Editor: Julia Bird
Designer: DR Ink
Art Director: Jonathan Hair

Picture credits: Martin Bond/Still Pictures: 18;
Mark Boulton/Alamy: 13; Andrew Brookes/Corbis: front
cover bl; David Burton/Alamy: front cover br; Nigel
Cattlin/Alamy: 25; Lindsay Constable/Alamy: 19;
Vicki Coombs/Ecoscene: 10; Gustavo Fadel/Shutterstock:
12; Andrew Fox/Alamy: 20; Paul Glendell/Alamy: 9;
Goh Siok Hian/Shutterstock: 15; The Irish Image
Collection/Corbis: front cover t; Marek
Kulias/Shutterstock: 11b; Phillip Lange /Shutterstock: 24;
Connor Lee/Oberlin Living Machine/Wikipedia
Commons: 16; Stephen McSweeny /Shutterstock: 6;
Andrei Merkulov/Shutterstock: 11t; Francoise Sauze/SPL:
14; Ariel Skelly/Corbis: 7; Jo Ann Snover/Shutterstock: 22;
Anthony Jay D. Villalon/Shutterstock: 23;
S. Windjue/UWSP: 21; David Woodfall/Still Pictures: 17.

A CIP catalogue record for this book
is available from the British Library

ISBN: 978 1 4451 3032 3

Dewey Classification: 363.72'84

Printed in China

Franklin Watts is a division of
Hachette Children's Books,
an Hachette UK company.
www.hachette.co.uk

Contents

Water and waste

● Water at home

People, animals and plants all need water to grow and live. Every day, we use water to drink, wash and cook, keep our homes and cars clean, and care for gardens and pets.

● Water at work

We also need water for farms, factories and **power stations**. We use water to grow crops and when we make everything from DVD players to T-shirts and shoes.

DID YOU KNOW?

We use about 9.5 litres of water every time we flush the toilet.

It takes 5,000 litres of water to produce 1 kilogram of potatoes.

● Wasting water

We flush away about a third of our drinkable water. If we leave a tap running when we clean our teeth, we can waste as much as 5 litres of water a minute. Rainwater is also wasted when it runs off roofs, roads and driveways. All of this water can be **recycled**.

JUST THE FACTS

How we use water in the home:
- Washing ourselves: 33%
- Washing clothes and cars, cooking, using dishwashers and watering gardens: 33%
- Flushing toilets: 33%.

Leaving the tap running while cleaning your teeth wastes a lot of water.

Why recycle water?

● Freshwater

Water covers three-quarters of the Earth, but most of it is in the salty seas and oceans. Only 1% of the world's water is **freshwater** that we can drink, so it is important that we recycle all the water we can.

● The water cycle

Earth's water is recycled every day. The Sun heats up water in lakes, rivers and seas and turns it into **water vapour**. As the vapour cools, it forms clouds and falls back to Earth as rain, hail or snow.

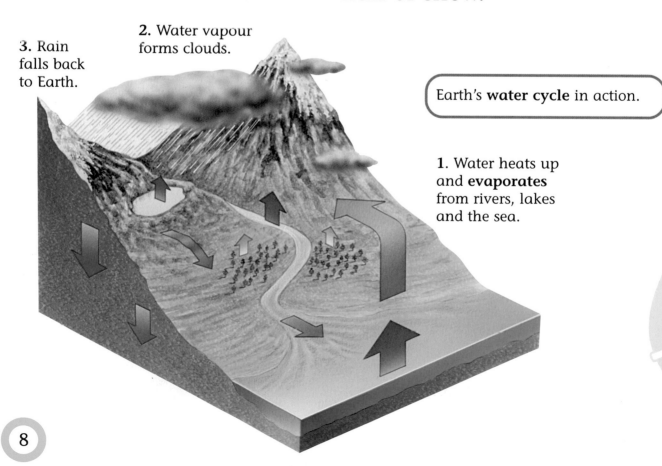

3. Rain falls back to Earth.

2. Water vapour forms clouds.

Earth's **water cycle** in action.

1. Water heats up and **evaporates** from rivers, lakes and the sea.

8

Growing demand

As the world's **population** grows, there is less water to go around. Even though the UK has more rain than many countries, the south east region has less water available per person than hot, dry countries such as Syria and the Sudan.

Climate change

In the future, **climate change** will mean that parts of the world have more **droughts**. There will also be more storms and floods, but these can make sewers overflow, **polluting** drinking water.

The 2007 floods in England polluted local water supplies. People had to use bottled water for several days.

Sewage recycling

● Screening

In most households, the water we use at home runs into drains and becomes **sewage** water. This is recycled at sewage treatment plants. First, the water is **screened** to remove bits of waste. It then passes through tanks where **oxygen** bubbles help grit to settle so that it can be pumped out and sent to **landfill**.

Sewage water is screened first to remove toilet paper and large bits of waste.

● Digesters

The solid waste settles in the tanks as sludge which is piped into **digesters**. These are giant tanks in which **bacteria** break down or digest the waste. The digested waste can be turned into pellets or liquid and used as **fertiliser** on farms.

Filtering

The liquid waste passes into tanks where giant rakes **skim** off any oil, soaps or plastics that float to the top. The waste then passes through sand or carbon filters to kill germs and smells.

JUST THE FACTS

Some sewage recycling plants can treat up to 40 million litres of water each day.

Solid waste is piped away into big digesters like these.

Treated water is pumped into rivers to be taken back into the water supply.

Cleaning

Finally, the water is treated with **ultraviolet** light or chemicals to kill any remaining **germs**. The water is then safe to be used as drinking water.

Grey water

● Used water

There are many other ways of saving or re-using water at home. **Grey water** is water that has been used in basins, baths or showers. It must be cleaned and treated before it can be used again. It will still not be clean enough to drink, but it can be used to flush toilets, wash clothes or water gardens.

GREEN GUIDE

When you re-use water you save **energy** too, because pumping water to homes uses energy.

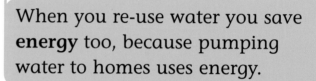

Soapy bath water can be cleaned and re-used.

Grey water tanks

Homes can have grey water tanks fitted. The water is collected from kitchens and bathrooms and pumped into special tanks.

JUST THE FACTS

Grey water can replace up to a third of household water usage.

Grey water tanks can save householders money by reducing water bills.

Cleaning

The first tank has **filters** to remove hair and other bits of waste. The water then passes into a tank where bacteria feed on any **organic** matter and oxygen is pumped through to help clean it. Next, the water passes into a tank where ultraviolet light kills any germs. The clean water is tested, then pumped to toilets, washing machines and outside taps.

Harvesting rainwater

● Storage

Some people fit systems to **harvest** rainwater at home. It can be used for flushing toilets or to water gardens in dry weather. The rain is collected from roofs in **gutters** and sent down pipes that carry it to underground tanks or **water butts**.

JUST THE FACTS

Rainwater can replace over half a home's water supply.

Rainwater butts can be used to collect the water that runs off the roofs of houses, garages or even greenhouses.

Cleaning

Rainwater can be used straight from water butts for the garden. For indoor use, it must be cleaned and treated. Filters in underground tanks remove any bits of grit or waste and oxygen is pumped through the water to clean it.

The rainwater stored in a water butt can be used to water the garden during dry weather.

? DID YOU KNOW?

You need to use less soap and shampoo when you wash with rainwater, as it is softer than tap water.

Household use

The treated rainwater can be pumped to toilets, washing machines and outside taps. If the level of water in the tank becomes low, the householder can switch to **mains** water.

Living Machines®

Recycling tanks

Living Machines® are another way that some householders recycle water at home. They are a system of tanks that can be used to recycle rain, grey water and sewage water for toilet flushing and outdoor taps. They can supply a house or even whole villages with water.

Living Machines® use natural processes to clean grey water.

Living Machines® clean water in the same way as **reed beds**, like this one in Cambridgeshire.

Cleaning

Living Machines® tanks contain reeds and other water plants. Their stems help waste to settle and their roots release oxygen into the water, encouraging bacteria to grow and feed on the waste. In each tank, plants and bacteria, as well as fish, snails and other water creatures also feed on the waste, cleaning the water.

Storage

The clean water is stored in underground tanks before being pumped to homes for flushing toilets or watering the garden.

?

DID YOU KNOW?

Reed beds are important **habitats** for birds, fish and other forms of wildlife.

Green roofs

● Storing rainwater

Green roofs are another way of helping us to use water more efficiently. These are roofs that have been adapted to grow plants which can store and **filter** rainwater.

● Top and bottom

The roof is prepared in layers to support the plants and protect the building. The bottom layers of the roof help to filter and drain water away. On top is a layer in which plants can take root and grow.

This modern 'eco-house' has a green roof.

● Filtering roots

The plant roots take in rain as it falls on the roof and filter and clean it. Green roofs also suck up dust and dirt from the air, reduce the level of noise from outside and keep buildings warm in winter and cool in summer.

?

DID YOU KNOW?

Green roofs can be home to up to 40 different types of insects.

Any water that runs off green roofs can be collected and used to flush toilets or water gardens.

Storm water

● Run off

Storm water is caused by heavy rain or melted snow running off roads, car parks and other paved surfaces. Storm water **run off** can make drains and sewers overflow, causing flooding and polluting rivers and other water sources.

● Storm water tanks

Storm water can be collected by gutters and sent down pipes to run into tanks under houses or gardens. The stored water can be used to water plants or clean cars, or it can be treated and used to flush toilets.

Rain storms can cause flooding when drains and sewers overspill.

Rain gardens

Storm water can also be collected in **rain gardens**. Rain gardens are dug into the ground to collect run off from paved surfaces, such as roofs, driveways and gardens. They use gravel, sand or **mulch** that allow rain to soak through them to re-fill underground **aquifers**. The plants also help to take up storm water through their roots.

Rain gardens are usually planted with **native** plants as they are best suited to the **environment**.

Making freshwater

Salty water

As the world's freshwater is in short supply, scientists have found a way of turning saltwater into freshwater using a process called **desalination**.

Desalination plants pump in water from the sea and remove the salt. This can be done by heating and evaporating the water or by pumping it through filters.

Desalination plants are located near coasts.

Filtering

The water is treated to remove any bits of waste, then it is pumped through filters that separate it into two streams. One is freshwater and the other is very salty. **Minerals** and chemicals are added to the freshwater to kill any germs. The water is tested, then piped to homes.

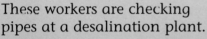
These workers are checking pipes at a desalination plant.

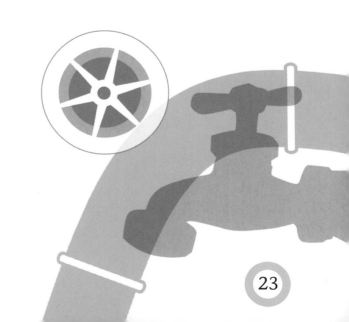

Waste water energy

Biogas

Waste and sewage water can be turned into energy. They are piped to plants where they are treated in digesters. Inside, bacteria feed on the sewage and other waste, releasing **biogas**. Biogas contains **methane** and **carbon dioxide** and it can be burned to make electricity. The digesters also produce solid or liquid waste called **digestate**, which can be used as fertiliser on farmland.

Giant tanks at a biogas plant.

● Saving energy costs

Water companies can treat sewage waste to make their own energy. They heat and dry the sewage, then feed it to bacteria. The biogas is used to save energy costs at the plant, and digestate is sold to farms.

GREEN GUIDE

Biogas is a renewable form of energy, which means it won't run out like oil or coal.

JUST THE FACTS

In France and Sweden, some buses run on biogas.

Digestate can be used on farms as a crop fertiliser.

What you can do

CASE STUDY

Children at Wattle Park Primary School in Melbourne are used to saving water because of drought. They use timers to take 2-minute showers and catch the water in buckets. Monitors at school check that water from running taps is collected in buckets and used to water the school's vegetable garden.

5 top tips for water recyclers:

1
Use butts, bowls and buckets to collect rainwater.

2
Re-use water from pet bowls or fish tanks for plants.

3
Use grey water in the garden.

4
Rinse jars and bottles in used washing-up water before recycling them.

5
Above all, try to reduce the amount of water you use.

Filtering grey water

You will need:

A bowl of grey water
(eg from a sink or basin)

An old sock or stocking
A watering can

Step 1
Use a bowl to collect used washing-up water in a sink or basin.

Step 2
Fit the sock or stocking over the spout of the watering can.

Step 3
Carefully pour the water from the bowl into the watering can.

Step 4
Use the can to water your plants. The sock or stocking filter should trap most of the soapy sludge, but don't use grey water on plants that you are going to eat.

Glossary

Aquifers Underground stores of water.

Bacteria Tiny living things; some are helpful, some are not.

Biogas A type of gas, containing methane and carbon dioxide, that can be used to make electricity.

Carbon dioxide A gas found in the air.

Climate change A gradual change in the Earth's climate, caused by gases from cars and industry.

Desalination Removing salt.

Digestate Solid or liquid waste produced by digesters.

Digesters Tanks for breaking down organic waste.

Droughts Long periods of time without rain.

Energy Heat or power.

Environment Surroundings.

Evaporates Turns from a liquid into a vapour.

Fertiliser A substance used to improve soil.

Filters Devices that screen or sieve substances.

Freshwater Water that is not salty.

Germs Harmful bacteria, many of which can cause disease.

Green roofs Roofs that have been adapted to grow grass and other plants.

Grey water Water that has been used in baths, showers or basins.

Gutters Channels at the edge of roofs or roads for carrying water away.

Habitats The natural environments of living things.

Harvest Gather or collect.

Landfill Places where rubbish is buried under the ground.

Living Machines® The name for a system of water recycling using tanks and plants.

Mains The main water supply network.

Methane A type of gas that is given off when natural substances break down.

Minerals Natural substances that we need to stay healthy.

Mulch A covering for soil or plants.

Organic Able to break down naturally.

Oxygen A gas found in air that living things need to stay alive.

Native Belonging to a particular place.

Pollute When harmful substances get into the soil, water or air.

Population The total number of people living in a place.

Power stations Places where electricity is generated.

Rain gardens Gardens dug into the ground to collect run off.

Recycled When something, such as a material, is used again.

Reed beds A type of wetland where reeds grow.

Run off Water that runs off hard surfaces.

Screened Passed through a sieve or screen.

Sewage The waste that is carried away in sewers or drains.

Sewers Drain or pipes that carry away water and sewage.

Skim To remove floating matter from a liquid.

Storm water Water from heavy rain or snow or ice melt.

Ultra violet A type of light ray.

Water butts Tubs or barrels for collecting rainwater.

Water cycle The way in which water from sea, lakes and rivers returns to Earth in the form of rain, hail or snow.

Water vapour Water in the air.

Further information

Books

Our World of Water Zadie Smith, Frances Lincoln 2009

Reduce, Re-use, Recycle: Water Jen Green, Wayland 2009

Waste Water (Dealing with Waste) Sally Morgan, Franklin Watts, 2006

Websites

www.savetherain.info

Information on rainwater harvesting.

www.waterwise.org.uk

Lots of water saving tips and ideas.

www.waterfootprint.org

A website all about the amount of water we use in different ways.

Note to parents and teachers: Every effort has been made by the Publishers to ensure that the websites in this book are suitable for children, that they are of the highest educational value, and that they contain no inappropriate or offensive material. However, because of the nature of the Internet, it is impossible to guarantee that the contents of these sites will not be altered. We strongly advise that Internet access is supervised by a responsible adult.

Index